A Primary Source Guide to the

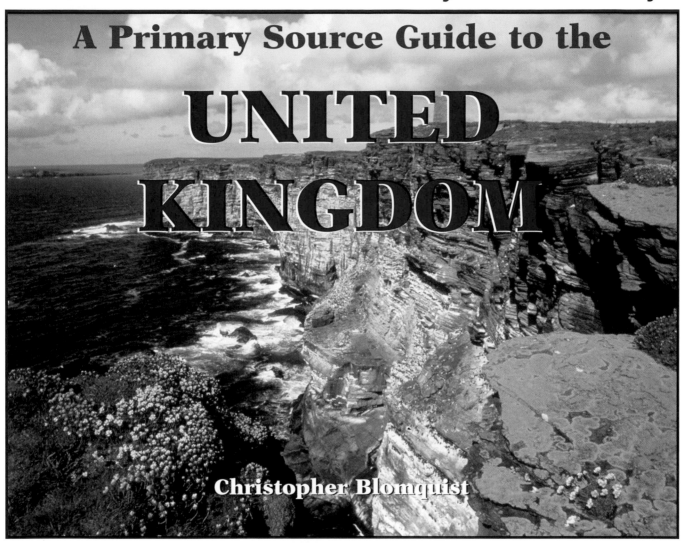

UNITED KINGDOM

Christopher Blomquist

The Rosen Publishing Group's

PowerKids Press™
PRIMARY SOURCE

New York

For Edina and Ian

Published in 2005 by The Rosen Publishing Group, Inc.
29 East 21st Street, New York, NY 10010

Copyright © 2005 by The Rosen Publishing Group, Inc.

First Edition

Editor: Kathy Kuhtz Campbell
Book Design: Haley Wilson
Layout Design: Michael J. Caroleo
Photo Researcher: Adriana Skura

Photo Credits: Cover Image © Allan, D.Osf/Earth Scenes; p. 6 © Michael Busselle/Corbis, (inset) © Robert Maier/Earth Scenes; p. 8 © Mike Slater/Earth Scenes, (inset) Gianni Dagli Orti/Corbis; p. 9 © HIP/Scala/Art Resource, NY; p. 10 © Ric Ergenbright/Corbis; p. 12 © Reuters NewMedia Inc/Corbis; p. 14 © Adam Woolfitt/Corbis, (inset) © Eranian Philippe/Corbis Sygma; p. 16 © Angelo Hornak/Corbis, (inset) © The Pierpoint Morgan Library/Art Resource, NY; p. 18 © Everett Collection; p. 19 © Chris Hellier/Corbis; p. 20 © London Aerial Photo Library/Corbis.

Library of Congress Cataloging-in-Publication Data
Blomquist, Christopher.
A primary source guide to the United Kingdom / Christopher Blomquist.— 1st ed.
        p. cm. — (Countries of the world, a primary source journey)
Summary: Text and photographs depict the history, government, culture, and traditions of the United Kingdom, the birthplace of the Industrial Revolution.
Includes bibliographical references and index.
ISBN 1-4042-2760-1 (lib. bdg.)
1. Great Britain—Juvenile literature. 2. Northern Ireland—Juvenile literature. [1. Great Britain. 2. Northern Ireland.] I. Title. II. Series.
DA27.5 .B59 2005
941—dc22
                                            2003018190

Manufactured in the United States of America

Contents

Atlantic
Ocean

Shetland
Islands

Orkney
Islands

NORWAY

Isle of Lewis

BRITISH
ISLES

SCOTLAND

△ Ben Nevis

North
Sea

Edinburgh

United
Kingdom

NORTHERN
IRELAND

Belfast ■

Isle of
Man

GERMANY

Leeds
Manchester

*Irish
Sea*

IRELAND

ENGLAND

Birmingham

NETHERLANDS

WALES

London ■

Cardiff ■

Canterbury

BELGIUM

Isle of
Wight

English Channel

Channel
Islands

FRANCE

4

A Nation of Islands

The United Kingdom is part of the British Isles in northwestern Europe off Europe's **mainland**. The United Kingdom includes the countries of England, Scotland, and Wales, together with the six counties of Northern Ireland. These are joined under one government. The country's full name is the United Kingdom of Great Britain and Northern Ireland.

Great Britain, which is often called Britain, includes England in the south, Wales in the west, and Scotland in the north. Northern Ireland is to the west of England, across the Irish Sea, on the northeastern part of the island of Ireland. The **Republic** of Ireland, a separate nation, makes up the rest of this island.

The United Kingdom includes Scotland, England, Wales, and Northern Ireland. It also includes nearby islands, such as the Shetland Islands, the Orkney Islands, and the Isle of Wight.

A Rainy Land

The United Kingdom has mountain ranges in the north and west and lower land in the central, southern, and eastern areas. The eastern areas of England are flat but there are hills in northern, central, and southern England. The British Isles also have wetland areas called moors. Northern Scotland has rocky, tall mountains including Ben Nevis, the United Kingdom's highest peak at 4,406 feet (1,343 m).

Warm, wet ocean air makes the United Kingdom a rainy place. On average, it rains every other day. Scotland's western coast is the wettest area, getting as much as 100 inches (254 cm) of rain per year.

◄ Sheep and cattle are raised in Romney Marsh, in the county of Kent in southeastern England. *Inset*: Cliffs rise from the North Sea at St. Abb's Head, located on Scotland's southeastern coast.

ONTRA   DINA NT

8

No one knows when people first came to the British Isles. However, around 4500 B.C. groups of people, using stone tools and weapons, began to settle in Britain. They grew crops and raised animals. About 400 B.C. a warrior people, the Celts, moved to Britain from mainland Europe. The Romans ruled England from A.D. 43 to A.D. 410. Then groups of Germanic and Scandinavian peoples took over. In 1066, William the **Conqueror** from Normandy, France, beat King Harold II of England at the Battle of Hastings. In 1215, nobles forced England's king John I to sign the Magna Carta, which curbed the king's power.

About 5,000 years ago, the Iberians built Stonehenge. The huge stone circle is located on Salisbury Plain in southern England. *Inset:* The *Bayeux Tapestry*, a wall hanging, shows events about William the Conquerer's attack on England. *Above:* The Magna Carta required rulers to recognize the laws of the land.

A United Kingdom

The United Kingdom did not reach its present form until 1921. England united, or joined, with Wales in 1536 and with Scotland in 1707. Ireland, which England conquered in 1650, became Ireland and Northern Ireland in 1921. Northern Ireland remained part of the United Kingdom. The rest of the island officially became independent in 1949.

Today the United Kingdom is a **constitutional monarchy**. This means that the ruler has little real power. The government's leader is called a prime minister. The prime minister's cabinet, or advisers, and a **parliament** run the government. Parliament is made up of the House of Commons and the House of Lords.

The United Kingdom's government meets in these buildings, called the Houses of Parliament, in London, England. Parliament makes the laws. It includes the 659 members of the House of Commons as well as the House of Lords, which has about 600 members. This view also shows the clock tower that houses Big Ben.

The British Empire

During Queen Elizabeth I's rule, from 1558 to 1603, England started its overseas exploration. It began to set up colonies around the world, such as Virginia in North America in 1584. In 1783, England's 13 North American colonies won their freedom and became the United States. However, England owned, or later gained control of, other lands, such as Canada, Australia, and parts of Asia and Africa. In the 1800s and the 1900s, the British **Empire** included two-fifths of the world's land and one-quarter of its people. It was said that the sun never set on the British Empire, for at any given hour it was daytime in at least one place that the British controlled.

This painting of Queen Elizabeth I honors the British navy's beating of Spain's navy, called the Armada, in 1588. When Britain's destroyed the Spanish Armada, Britain became the world's greatest sea power.

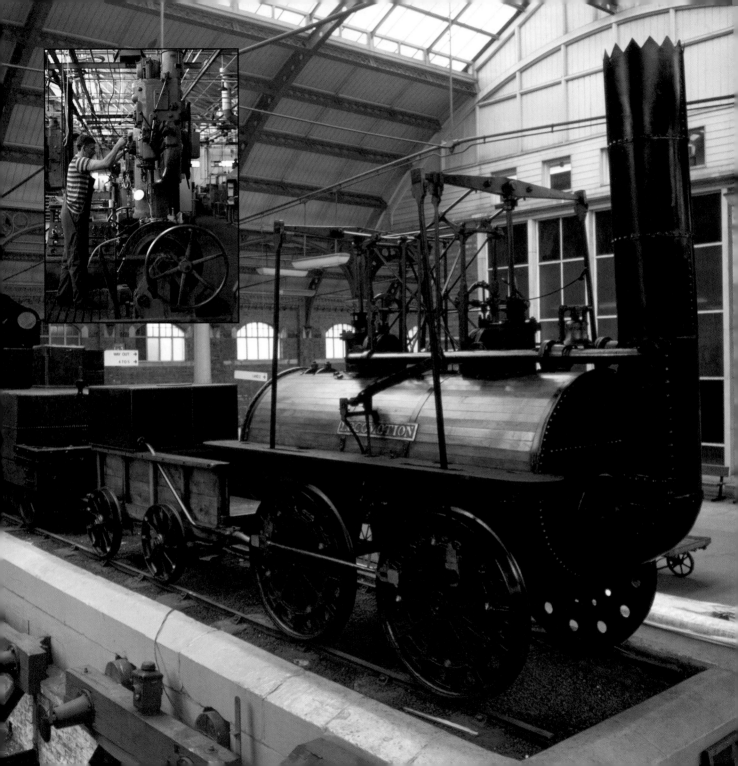

The United Kingdom's Economy

The United Kingdom was the birthplace of the **Industrial Revolution**, which occurred between 1750 and 1850. It was the first nation to make the majority of its products by machine in factories instead of by hand on farms or in homes. By the mid-1800s, the new factories produced items such as cotton, iron, and steel. These factories also produced goods made from these items, such as cloth or machine parts. The factories changed the United Kingdom from a country dependent on farming to the leading manufacturer and seller of industrial goods. Towns such as Birmingham, Leeds, and Manchester in England became important for their factories and wool and cotton mills.

This photo shows *Locomotion 1*, the first steam-powered train used on a public railway. English inventor George Stephenson made it in 1825. *Inset:* In 1995, a laborer works a machine in a Rolls Royce factory in Manchester, England.

Religion in the United Kingdom

Until the 1530s, England was a **Roman Catholic** country. King Henry VIII, who ruled from 1509 to 1547, wanted to end his marriage. The Catholic Church would not allow it. In 1534, he formed the Church of England, a **Protestant** church, which let him end his marriage. Henry made the Church of England the national religion and became its official head.

Today the United Kingdom's population is mostly Protestant. The Church of England and Scotland's **Presbyterian** Church are the established religions of those areas. Wales and Northern Ireland do not have established religions. Non-Christian religions practiced in Britain include **Islam**, **Hinduism**, and **Judaism**.

At Canterbury Cathedral in southeastern England, the archbishop of Canterbury serves as the religious head of the Church of England. *Inset: This is the title page from the Bible that was printed in 1611, during England's king James I's rule.*

Writing and Music

The United Kingdom has produced some of the world's finest writers and popular music. William Shakespeare lived from 1564 to 1616. His works are still read and performed worldwide and include plays such as *Romeo and Juliet* and *Hamlet*. Charles Dickens, who lived from 1812 to 1870, is another well-known British author. One of his books, *A Christmas Carol*, tells the story of how a mean man discovers the true meaning of Christmas.

The country also changed popular music in the 1960s, when a rock band called the Beatles had many hit songs around the world. Other popular singers include Elton John and Sting.

The Beatles, a four-man rock band from Liverpool, England, appeared on American television on June 1, 1966. Their hit songs include "Yellow Submarine" and "Let It Be." *Above*: This picture of William Shakespeare appeared around 1623, in the first printing of a collection of his plays.

Elizabeth Blackwell Elementary

£5 BANK OF ENGLAND £5 £5

FIVE POUNDS

1780 - 1845

The United Kingdom Today

At the end of World War II in 1945, the United Kingdom's economy was very weak and most of its colonies became independent. Today the country and its economy are strong again. It is a member of the **United Nations** and the **European Union**.

Prime Minister Tony Blair, elected in 1997, brought important changes to the government. He reduced the number of nonelected nobles in the House of Lords. In addition, Scotland, Wales, and Northern Ireland have been given more local power in recent years. Although the United Kingdom is no longer a huge empire, it is a powerful nation. Its past is interesting and its future is bright.

This view of London, England, was taken in 2000. London, the capital of the United Kingdom since the fourteenth century, is a banking and trade center for the world. *Inset*: The pound sterling is the United Kingdom's national money. The country has not replaced its money with that of the European Union's euro.

21

The United Kingdom at a Glance

Population: 59,778,002

Capital City: London

Largest City: London, population 7,285,000

Official Name: United Kingdom of Great Britain and Northern Ireland

National Anthem: "God Save the Queen"

Land Area: 94,248 square miles (244,101 sq km)

Government: Constitutional monarchy

Unit of Money: Pound sterling

Flag: The United Kingdom's flag is called the Union Jack. The word "jack" means "flag." It has a red cross on a white background, a white X on a blue background, and a red X on a white background.

Glossary

conqueror (KON-ker-er) A person who wins something by force.

constitutional monarchy (kon-stih-TOO-shu-nul MAH-nar-kee) A government in which a country has both a ruler and elected leaders.

empire (EM-pyr) A large area controlled by one ruler.

European Union (yur-uh-PEE-in YOON-yun) A group of countries in Europe that work together to be friendly and to better their businesses.

Hinduism (HIN-doo-ih-zum) A faith that was started in India.

Industrial Revolution (in-DUS-tree-ul reh-vuh-LOO-shun) A time in the mid-1700s when power-driven machines were first used to produce goods in large quantities, changing the way people lived and worked.

Islam (IS-lom) A faith based on Muhammad's teachings and the Koran.

Judaism (JOO-dee-ih-zum) The faith followed by Jews, based on teachings in the Torah.

mainland (MAYN-land) A large area of land near an island.

parliament (PAR-lih-mint) The lawmakers of the United Kingdom.

Presbyterian (prez-bih-TEER-ee-un) Having to do with a branch of the Christian church.

Protestant (PRAH-tes-tunt) Having to do with a Christian-based religion.

republic (ree-PUB-lik) A form of government in which people elect representatives who run the government.

Roman Catholic (ROH-mun KATH-lik) Of the Christian faith that recognizes the pope as its head.

United Nations (yoo-NY-ted NAY-shunz) A worldwide group formed at the end of World War II in 1945 to keep peace between nations.

Index

Primary Source List

Cover. Marwick Head, Kitchener Memorial and Royal Society for the Protection of Birds Reserve, Orkney, Scotland. The memorial was built to honor Lord Kitchener and the crew of the HMS *Hampshire*, which was sunk on June 5, 1916, by a German mine off the coast of the southern end of Birsay Bay during World War I.

Page 8. Stonehenge, built around 3000 B.C., possibly as a place of worship to the Sun, in Wiltshire, Wessex, England.

Page 8 (inset). Detail of *William I Attacking Dinan with His Army* from the *Bayeux Tapestry*. Wool embroidery on linen, height 20 inches (51 cm), total length of tapestry is about 230 feet (70 m). Town Hall, Bayeux. Made around 1073–83. The tapestry shows William the Conqueror's invasion of England, from the events in France leading up to the Battle of Hastings.

Page 9. The Magna Carta. This is the third version of the Magna Carta, issued in 1225 by Henry III. Public Record Office, London, England.

Page 12. *The Armada Portrait of Elizabeth I* is believed to have been painted by George Gower around 1588 or 1589. It is in the collection of Woburn Abbey in Bedfordshire, England. Another version of the Armada Portrait is in the collection of the National Portrait Gallery, London.

Page 14. George Stephenson's *Locomotive 1* pulled the first steam train along an 1825 railway route. Darlington Railway Museum, England.

Page 16. Canterbury Cathedral, photographed between 1971 and 1996. The cathedral was founded in 597 by St. Augustine, the first archbishop of Canterbury. It was destroyed by fire twice, in 1067 and in 1174, and the central part of the building dates from the late fourteenth century.

Page 16 (inset). Title page to the New Testament, from the King James Bible, printed in London in 1611. The Pierpont Morgan Library, New York.

Page 19. *Portrait of Playwright William Shakespeare*. Engraving by Martin Droeshout. First Folio edition of William Shakespeare's plays, about 1623.

Page 20. Title page, the New Testament, from the King James Bible. Printed in London by Robert Barker in 1611. The Pierpont Morgan Library, NY.

Web Sites

Due to the changing nature of Internet links, PowerKids Press has developed an online list of Web sites related to the subject of this book. This site is updated regularly. Please use this link to access the list:

www.powerkidslinks.com/cwpsj/psuk/